PARACHUTES
OVER
BRITAIN

PARACHUTES OVER BRITAIN

by
JOHN LANGDON-DAVIES

The Naval & Military Press Ltd

Published by

The Naval & Military Press Ltd
Unit 5 Riverside, Brambleside
Bellbrook Industrial Estate
Uckfield, East Sussex
TN22 1QQ England

Tel: +44 (0)1825 749494

www.naval-military-press.com
www.nmarchive.com

*In reprinting in facsimile from the original, any imperfections are inevitably reproduced
and the quality may fall short of modern type and cartographic standards.*

*To the Defenders of Burwash and
a thousand other British villages*

CONTENTS

Chapter I

From Napoleon to Hitler	....	....	9
Sir John Moore to the Rescue	....	....	11

Chapter II

The Parachute	....	....	....	16
The Menace	....	....	....	21
What should We expect?		....	....	24
The Fifth Column	....	....	....	27
The Parachutists	....	....	....	29

Chapter III

The Enemy's Plan of Action	....	....	32
The Basis of Successful Defence		....	33
The Arming of the People	....	....	34

Contents

Chapter IV

A Nation of Observers	37
Sending in Reports	40
Strangers on the Road	43

Chapter V

Mass Parachute Action	47
Barricades	47
Village Barricades	51
Street Defence	53
Keep Communications Open	54
Guard Against Troop-carrying Planes	56
Invasion and the War as a Whole	58

CHAPTER I

From Napoleon to Hitler

I WRITE these notes in a Sussex garden. Two miles away on the skyline I can see a rough stone monument marking the spot on which a great beacon would have been lit, if Napoleon had invaded England in about 1803.

A few miles beyond this monument is Hastings, and the scene of the last successful invasion of our shores —1066 And All That. Within a stone's-throw of the monument to-day there is a barricade of ancient farm implements, bricks and stone, and barbed wire, guarded by two young men in their early twenties, complete with steel helmets, rifles and bayonets.

Over the hill behind my back, concealed behind a dip, is an army field dressing station. Every few miles along all the roads to left and right there are barricades. In the village pub to-night most of us are meeting to discuss the formation of a local Defence Corps of Parashots. Perhaps by the time these words appear in print England will have been seriously invaded again, the first time for 834 years.

Let us look at the steps taken during the French Revolutionary Wars to prepare against a French inva-

PARACHUTES OVER BRITAIN

sion. The first was to build Martello Towers, circular defensible works, which may still be seen in quantity on the Kent and Sussex coast. Then, in 1801, a full scheme for Home Defence was worked out: not much of it is applicable to our problem to-day.

The enemy's objective was defined as the invasion of our coasts, probably at several different points, in order to attack and paralyse London as the centre of our kingdom. To-day the German objective is to invade, and to keep us guessing the point at which the invasion will be. That is one reason why they secured Southern Norway before attacking the French Channel ports.

We cannot possibly tell at what point from the north of Scotland to Southampton the blow or blows will fall. Throughout this area every male inhabitant must be on the watch, must be trained to observe and report anything that he sees, must know how to harass and hold up the enemy until adequate military forces can arrive.

One of the grimmest necessities then laid down in the instructions is as follows:—Defence Commanders were to take steps towards " hastening the inhabitants in the neighbourhood of the enemy to withdraw their cattle and horses, to enforce this by every means, and to destroy, without compunction, whatever provision is tardy in its removal or could be of use to him . . . from the moment that an enemy is discovered from the coast and pointing to a place of landing, the driving of the country must begin, be strongly enforced and made, if possible, by other routes than those of probable operation of the troops, whose movements must not be interrupted; and when the acting direction of the enemy is sufficiently ascertained, nothing within the probability of his reach should be suffered to remain . . . above all, the removal of horses of every description must be accomplished . . . nothing will more effectually disconcert the project of an invading enemy than the driving and abandonment of the country and the total destruction of the roads for miles round. . . ."

In short, the instructions of our authorities in 1801 were to meet the threat of an invasion by falling back on the defensive at once. It is interesting to note that the point of view which has been the cause of so much that has gone wrong in the present war was orthodox then as now.

Sir John Moore to the Rescue

It took a great soldier, Sir John Moore, to point out that it was neither useful nor possible to turn the fair shires of England into wasteland, that, instead of cluttering up the roads with masses of fleeing cattle, they must be kept free for masses of attacking soldiers, that only by abandoning defeatist defensiveness and being thoroughly offensive could one meet an invasion.

Parachutes Over Britain

If these instructions had been carried out, the French invaders would have been able to isolate our forces in their Martello Towers, to march right through their lines, and occupy the country inland long before it could be sufficiently laid waste to make it an obstacle to further progress.

That is exactly what would happen to-day if we were to imagine for a moment that we could repel an invader with the floating fortresses of our Navy, or that we should be content with removing our motor-cars and horses, and evacuating the population, and hoping that the military would arrive in time to deal with the problem.

There is only one way to repel an invasion, as Sir John Moore saw then, and as we have seen just in time now, and that is to arm the people of England.

" Horses and wagons," wrote Sir John Moore, " alone should be removed." In the same way to-day motor-cars and bicycles must not be left about for the use of invaders. " In the coast countries," Sir John Moore went on, " every man capable of work, or bearing arms, must be enrolled, and belong to some association, company, patrol, or whatever name is preferred. Every man will thus know his leaders, who, of course, will be the neighbouring gentlemen and better sort of farmers, and his place of rendezvous. The county, thus organized, is never to assemble, but when the enemy is in sight, to

SIR JOHN MOORE TO THE RESCUE

fight for their own country, not to be marched into any other. Signals of alarm established, and universally known, upon which every man runs to his post. Depots of arms and ammunition lodged in various parts. Every man to go to his alarm post with two or three days' provisions. This force, when assembled, to be under the direction of the General Officer Commanding. . . . The language and the system should be to head and to oppose, and no foot of ground ceded that was not marked with the blood of the enemy. . . .

" Nothing would damp his spirit more than to see the country turned out against him. He knows the strength of our army—regular, militia, and reserve—and will come prepared to meet, and may hope to beat, it; but how penetrate or subdue a country where the population are armed and opposed to him?"

Almost every word of this is true to-day. The only difference is that there can be no waiting until the enemy is in sight. He will have made his landing, several miles inland perhaps, within fifteen minutes of taking off from his base behind Calais and Dunkirk.

" The bill for arming people, if carried into effect, will ensure success in the first instance. It will, at all events, enable us to wait at the point attacked, with the certainty of powerful and immediate support."

In a short while 342,000 men have been enrolled,

while Sir John Moore travelled up and down the counties speaking at public meetings to rouse the enthusiasm of the people. To-day, almost too late, we are doing the same.

According to Colonel J. F. C. Fuller, the volunteers had little resemblance with the description of a " partisan " given us some time before by a military writer.

" Of all military employments, there is none which requires more extraordinary qualities," wrote Roger Stevenson, " than that of the partisan. A good partisan ought to have an imagination fertile in projects, schemes, and resources; a penetrating spirit, capable of combining the whole circumstances of an action; a heart intrepid against every appearance of danger; a steady countenance, always assured, and which no sign of disquiet can alter; a happy memory, that can call everyone by his name; a disposition alert, to carry him through everything, and give a soul to the whole; a piercing, rapid eye, which instantly catches faults or advantages, obstacles and dangers of situation, of country and every object as it passes; his sentiments ought to be such as to fix the respect, confidence, and attachment of the whole corps. Without these dispositions it is impossible to succeed."

I do not know if the defence volunteers enrolling to-day see themselves like this. It is to be devoutly

SIR JOHN MOORE TO THE RESCUE

hoped that they do so. Those of us who, when younger, were Boy Scouts, or imagined ourselves to be Red Indians, have now got the opportunity to play our boyhood games on a grander scale.

CHAPTER II

The Parachute

As with so many other mechanical contrivances, the parachute occurred to the mind of Leonardo da Vinci, and at the beginning of the seventeenth century a Venetian gave a detailed description of a parachute shaped like an oblong canopy.

In the middle of the eighteenth century a French romance of adventure called " The Astral Discovery by a Flying Man, or the French Daedalus " appeared. The hero of this novel goes for world tours with artificial wings and an umbrella-shaped parachute fixed to his head.

In December, 1783, there took place the first recorded parachute jump. A Frenchman named Lenormand jumped safety to the ground from the Tower of Montpelier Observatory. His parachute outfit included a chair and a top hat.

A contemporary description of an event, which took place on October 22, 1797, may be translated as follows:
" On the 1st Brumaire of the Sixth Year of the Republic, Cifizen Garnerin ascended in a balloon from the Parc de Monceau. A deep silence reigned in the assembly and anxiety showed on all faces. When he reached the height of three thousand feet, he cut the cords which

held his parachute to the balloon—the latter exploded, and the parachute began to descend with such rapidity that a cry of horror escaped from the spectators, and several sensitive ladies fainted. But the parachute opened fully, and checked the speed of the descent.

" Citizen Garnerin reached the ground safely on the plain of Monceau, where he mounted a horse and returned to the Parc de Monceau. Here a stormy ovation greeted the talent and courage of the young aeronaut. In fact, Citizen Garnerin was the first who dared to undertake such a dangerous experiment. His success was announced to the Institut National, where it was received with great acclaim." Revolutionaries seem to be partial to the making of parachute history!

One of our illustrations shows that in 1803, when, as we have seen, French invasions were very much in the air, an imaginative strategist actually considered the possibility of supplementing sea forces by bringing the artillery through a Channel tunnel, and part of the infantry through the air in balloons, and suspended by kites. The print also shows a large incendiary bomb falling upon a ship.

About the same time, when the idea of flying was very much in the air, Goya engraved his magnificent print; but, apart from a humorist's suggestion that Scots soldiers might be sent from balloons, using their kilts as parachutes, nothing very much more than stunt descents at fairs took place until almost the beginning of the last Great War.

It is hard for those who do not remember **1914** to realize how infantile air warfare was in those days. The editor of " The Aeroplane " gave it as his considered opinion that planes would be exceedingly dangerous to troops below, especially if the pilots were provided with boxes of steel darts, which could be hurled down upon the enemy.

Planes were chiefly considered as the eyes of the army, and used for observation, and parachutes began to be given out to pilots simply to give the pilot a chance of rescuing himself when his plane got into difficulties.

It was not until after the Russian Revolution that the idea of using parachutes as a means of invading the enemy's country was first seriously taken up by the Red Army. The parachutists in the famous manœuvres, which so impressed foreign journalists and diplomatic representatives, were equipped with Tommy guns, and were trained to be able to get into small tanks also dropped by parachutes immediately upon landing, to start up their engines, and to race undisturbed far from the front lines to the capture of vital points in the enemy's rear.

It was known that the Germans were more impressed with this manœuvre than several other foreign countries, but I doubt if anybody was prepared for the wholesale

THE PARACHUTE

use of parachutists that we have seen since the invasion of Norway.

I have no record of parachutists being used in Spain, and their use in Finland was restricted. A certain number were used as spies and saboteurs. Probably most of these were Finnish exiled communists; but the Finnish military authorities rightly refused to give away any information at all as to their success, or lack of success. One of the most important rules to be observed in combatting the parachute menace is that absolutely no information should get back about their fate to the enemy.

I gathered that the parachutists in Finland did very little harm, but that they were extremely difficult to round up once they had landed. Bearing in mind the rigors of the climate, and the difficulties of the terrain, it is more than probable that some Russian parachutists frozen stiff have even yet not been discovered.

There were no recorded cases of successful sabotage; and the menace never developed farther than a vague cause for uneasiness. Towards the end, however, when the Russians were developing their mass attacks across the ice of the Gulf of Finland and west of Viipuri Bay, rather more parachutists were used, this time not as spies and saboteurs, but along the lines of the tactics displayed in the Moscow Red Army manœuvres: but events moved so rapidly to their appointed end, that here too there was no real opportunity of judging the value of parachutist invasion. The chief use of parachutes in Finland seems to have been as a means of laying mines from the air.

It was in Norway that the first real test came. Everybody knows how successful the parachutists proved. One hundred and twenty of them, armed with automatics, were able to capture the Sola airfield. Their success was largely due to co-operation with the Fifth Column.

In the invasion of Holland and Belgium this combination of Fifth Column and parachutist was much more thoroughly developed. An English witness has described the tactics:—Bombers, accompanied by fighters, came over in waves of 200 at a time, and at a very low altitude. The parachutists, to the number of perhaps twenty to a plane, seemed to have orders to make their way immediately to the principal buildings, which were pointed out by resident spies. It is alleged that some of them were dressed as butchers' and bakers' boys, and carried baskets filled with grenades and other ammunition over their arms, the ammunition being covered with a white cloth.

There are four parachute schools in Germany, where the technique of jumping and subsequent action is carefully taught. The art of correct jumping consists in judging the rate of wind and learning how to spill air from the canopy by pulling the shroud lines, and thus causing the parachute to side-slip in the right direction. The parachutists must bail out from the plane with the smallest possible interval between each one. They must be able to time accurately the length of their free fall before they pull their parachute open.

Their behaviour on landing must be carefully taught: they must have special qualifications for their task, a knowledge of the language of the country, skill in map reading and path finding, control of automatic weapons, and a specialized form of infantry training.

All sorts of things have been reported as part of their equipment, folding bicycles, and even small motorcycles, portable radios, camouflaged tents, as well as food, and the normal soldier's equipment.

A parachute weighs about eighteen pounds, complete with its harness. It slows up the descent to a fairly steady rate of sixteen-feet per second; but even then the shock of landing with so much equipment is considerable. Special spring boots are reported to be worn to take the shock.

The Menace

Mr. Anthony Eden has described the menace of invasion by parachute, and the need for a defence force in a recent broadcast speech. He said: " Let me say at once that the danger to us from this particular menace, although it undoubtedly exists, should not be exaggerated. We have made preparations to meet it already.

Parachutes Over Britain

" Let me describe to you the system under which these parachute raids are carried out. The troops arrive by aeroplane—but let it be remembered that any such aeroplane seeking to penetrate here would have to do so in the teeth of the anti-aircraft defences of this country.

" If such penetration is effected, the parachutists are then dropped, it may be by day, it may be by night. These troops are specially armed, equipped; and some of them have undergone specialized training. Their function is to seize important points, such as aerodromes, power stations, villages, railway junctions, and telephone exchanges, either for the purpose of destroying them at once, or of holding them until the arrival of reinforcements. The purpose of the parachute attack is to disorganize and confuse, as a preparation for the landing of troops by aircraft.

" The success of such an attack depends on speed. Consequently, the measures to defeat such an attack must be prompt and rapid. It is upon this basis that our plans have been laid.

" You will not expect me to tell you, or the enemy, what our plans are; but we are confident that they will be effective. However, in order to leave nothing to chance, and to supplement, from sources as yet untapped, the means of defence already arranged, we are going to ask you to help us, in a manner which I know will be welcomed to thousands of you. . . .

THE MENACE

"The name of the new force which is now to be raised will be the 'Local Defence Volunteers.' This name, Local Defence Volunteers, describes its duties in three words. It must be understood that this is, so to speak, a spare-time job, so there will be no need for any volunteer to abandon his present occupation.

". . . Now, a word to those who propose to volunteer. When on duty, you will form part of the Armed Forces, and your period of service will be for the duration of the war. You will not be paid; but you will receive uniform, and will be armed. You will be entrusted with certain vital duties, for which reasonable fitness and a knowledge of firearms are necessary. These duties will not require you to live away from your home. . . .

"This appeal is directed chiefly to those who live in small towns, villages, and less densely inhabited suburban areas. I must warn you that, for certain military reasons, there will be some localities where the numbers required will be small, and others where your services will not be required at all.

"Here, then, is the opportunity for which so many of you have been waiting. Your loyal help, added to the arrangements which already exist, will make and keep our country safe."

The following pages may be of assistance to those who have answered Mr. Eden's call.

Parachutes Over Britain

What should We expect?

It is no good remaining in a state of fear about some vague menace. The first step in dealing with a possible German invasion is to know exactly what the Germans can do, and what they cannot do, so that we can turn our general state of alarm, which merely weakens us, into a concrete anxiety that certain necessary steps shall be taken to meet a concrete danger.

Let us begin by comparing the task of invading Britain with the tasks so easily accomplished of invading Holland, and Denmark, and Norway. Quite rightly, we say that it would be far harder to invade us than to invade Holland and Denmark, because we are an island; but that does not mean that we have nothing to learn from the fate of these two countries.

Norway, on the other hand, had to be invaded over the sea; and we should frankly admit that even one generation ago proper use of the overwhelming sea power which we now possess would have prevented the German invasion of Norway. Clearly, times have changed.

It was in Holland and Norway that Hitler first used his *secret weapon*. This was not the super-armoured tank, though this also took us by surprise, but the Fifth Column.

The invasion of Holland and Norway was accomplished with such rapidity as made it possible for the

What Should We Expect

Germans to land not only men, but all those elements which are needed to carry out the highly successful offensive tactics, which in a few days have made all our orthodox defence tactics look as inadequate as a countryside of medieval castles.

All the successes so far claimed by the Germans have been due to the use of low-flying bombers, to take the place of heavy artillery and to blast the way for tanks, used as cavalry. Because these tanks are so heavily protected that normal anti-tank weapons are useless against them, the defence has had no way of resisting them. Although anti-tank guns can be successfully hidden from bombing planes it is almost impossible to hide the sort of artillery needed to stop these tanks; and so the tanks have advanced in a sort of vacuum created by the bombers, and there has been no stopping them.

It is in conjunction with this formidable attack on the ground that infantry armed with automatics have been parachuted far behind the front lines to positions where they could form themselves into fighting units, and, in combination with tanks, seize vital positions. In the wake of the parachutists have come thousands more infantry brought by troop-carrying planes, and landed at airfields secured in advance by the efforts of the Fifth Column.

Parachutes Over Britain

Let us briefly recapitulate the necessary parts in the modern German technique of invasion.

1. The Fifth Column, to seize airports and other vital points long enough to hold them until the coming of parachutists.

2. Parachutists, to hold these points sufficiently long to secure the landing of troop-carrying planes.

3. Troop-carrying planes, numerous enough to land in a short time thousands of infantrymen.

4. Along with all these, the low-flying bomber, instead of artillery, and the super-armoured tank smashing its way through.

Let us emphasize the significance of this fourth element. Its task is not merely to smash through a line of defence, as it did at Sedan, and on through the famous " 25-mile gap ": it is also a means of carrying the equivalent of artillery and other heavy material, which cannot be dropped from the air, so as to make counter-attack across the invaded country or district, far in the rear of the main battle lines, as difficult as possible.

Now, let us consider how far Britain is vulnerable to these four elements of the modern technique of invasion, and how far we have arranged for resistance.

The Fifth Column

There has only been one country defeated in recent years without the existence of an organized enemy within the gate. That country was Finland. If there had been Quislings in Finland, it would have been perfectly easy for Russia to have used the same sort of tactics in Finland as were used by the Germans in Norway.

This is not the place to discuss why there was no Fifth Column in Finland, beyond saying that there was no organizable body of discontent there. There were no Fascists largely, because the Russo-German pact was regarded by right-wing Finns as the selling out of their country by Germans to the hereditary enemy. There were no Communists, because an enlightened policy of social and economic legislation had done so much for the Finnish worker and peasant that he did not think that Russia had anything better to offer him. There was no Peace Pledge Union, because no Finn was ever a pacifist.

The situation is very different in England. We have Fascists, Communists, and Peace Pledgers. We have also an enormous number of refugees. How far should we be on our guard against each of these four groups? How far can we expect them to play the part of Hitler's secret weapon in the coming invasion of this country?

Parachutes Over Britain

We are not concerned here with the demoralizing effect of the first three groups on morale and the war effort. We are discussing the possibility of destroying bridges, seizing airfields, creating confusion; and in these tasks it is unfortunately probable that Hitler's best agents are to be found amongst the refugees, especially among the *bona fide* victims of the Dutch and Belgian invasions. That is why it has already been necessary to restrict the movement even of the most anti-Nazi victim of Hitler, and particularly to remove them from the southern and eastern areas, where the danger of invasion is perhaps greatest. Fortunately, those refugees who are the best friends of their foster country are the first to recognize the necessity of drastic action.

It is probably not too much to say that Hitler will have to invade England without relying on his secret weapon; that is, he will have no chance of the Fifth Column occupying vital points such as airports for the brief half-hour or so while he is in the very act of landing concentrated bodies of parachutists. We can make quite certain of this by interning the remaining potentially dangerous aliens of both sexes, and particularly by preventing any possible activities of Fifth Columnists amongst them in the areas likely to be involved in the plans for invasion.

THE PARACHUTISTS

There is, however, quite a grave danger to be expected from respectable British subjects, many of them in important positions, who, though they must lie low at present, may very well become defeatists if things go very badly indeed; but, if our secret services do their job reasonably well, the Fifth Column cannot function.

The Parachutists

If the Hitler tactics of invasion cannot rely upon the use of a Fifth Column, the parachutist has to take its place in the general scheme. Unless the parachutist can seize key points, and particularly airports, a mass invasion of Britain will not be possible, so long as sea power remains as securely in our hands as it seems to be at present.

There are two distinct ways in which parachutists may be used against this country: first, as suicide squads intent upon doing as much damage as possible in the short time before they are captured; second, as a real advance guard of an invading army intent upon holding vital points until their numbers can be largely increased by troop-carrying planes.

The idea of a suicide squad is picturesque and captures the imagination; but in reality it is far more likely that parachutists will only be used as the advance guard of a real invading force. Hitler is not going to waste time dropping a few men to blow up the gasworks of a country town, or to dislodge a few rails on a railway line. He is playing for far higher stakes, and, if he acts quickly enough, the element of surprise in the new tactics gives him so great an advantage that he is unlikely to waste time on minor objectives.

If we want to understand the position which we have to face, we should realize that already the German High Command has selected perhaps a dozen alternative landing grounds, and that they have their plans fully worked out, so that, within two or three hours of the first parachutes landing, important military objectives will be in the hands of thousands, rather than hundreds, of German soldiers.

If we consider the necessities of the new tactics of invasion, we can make a good guess as to the kind of locality in which the parachutists are most likely to arrive. They will not just be dumped on the British countryside to burn haystacks and bridges and march on London. First of all they will be the pioneers, preparing the way for troop-carrying planes. They will, therefore, appear near possible landing fields.

This does not mean simply one of the existing airports. It means any flat and unenclosed part of the south and east of Britain, anywhere, in fact, which can rapidly be made suitable for the safe landing of troop-carrying planes.

THE PARACHUTISTS

Further than this, we must remember that the mere landing of a few thousand troops from troop-carrying planes would not in itself be a valuable manœuvre, unless these troops can in their turn seize a locality suitable for the bringing in of all their heavy mechanized material, without which modern infantry can effect very little.

In short, we can be perfectly certain that the German High Command has already prepared plans for the landing of parachutists in flat, open country near an existing port, or a possible landing-place accessible to some kind of German transport capable of carrying certain supplies.

CHAPTER III

The Enemy's Plan of Action

It is probable that the Nazis will make synchronized attacks on the south and the east coasts. On the east coast they will attempt to combine the air attack with the landing of tanks by sea. On the south coast they will not be able to do this, because of the concentration of mines, torpedo boats, submarines, planes and shore batteries, which can be brought to bear in the narrow part of the channel; but they will not need to make the attempt. Once Boulogne and Calais are securely in their hands, they can develop their attack almost as if the barrier of the Channel did not exist.

Let us see how they can attack, for example, Dover. The first stage will be an intensive air bombardment, not of the port itself, but of the town, and any camps or bodies of troops in the neighbourhood. This bombardment will be on a very large scale indeed, and it will be immediately followed by the dropping of some thousands of parachutists inland, capable of cutting off the approaches to Dover on the land side, and of establishing themselves in a suitable place for the creation of landing-fields for troop-carrying planes.

Aeronauts as conceived by Francisco Goya. A superb etching executed at the time of the Napoleonic Wars.

Russian parachute troops inspected before flight, carry parachute in left hand.

Russian parachutists in training. Equal distance between each man enables troops to land within short range of one another.

England Invaded. A French print of 1803, showing attack b
Channel Tunnel. Balloon on left drop

y troop-carrying balloon, whilst reinforcements arrive through
s incendiary bombs on English warships.

Soviet Russian marine parachute mine shown at an exhibition of war-booty in Finland. The total height of this apparatus is 180 ft.

Parachutist descending. He pulls shroud-lines, spilling air out of silk, to direct his fall.

Massed parachute descent at Moscow air-display. The Germans used even greater numbers in Holland.

THE BASIS OF SUCCESSFUL DEFENCE

These troops will be armed with automatics, and they will be able to advance inland behind the protection of the modern equivalent of a creeping barrage, that is, behind the " vacuum " caused by the bombing planes.

It is no longer necessary to land artillery at Dover. In the place of artillery the heavy bombers will fly incessantly back and forth from their base at Calais. How far such an invasion can be carried will depend upon the speed with which tanks and fighters can break the bombers' barrage and the force of the advancing infantry. The task will be made more difficult by operations which will be carried out by the Germans at the same time as these.

The Basis of Successful Defence

Three main tasks must be accomplished by the British Defence, if the invasion is to fail.

1. The British Fleet must retain command of the sea; but at the same time it may have to be risked in order to diminish the impact of the invasion on the Channel ports. We cannot rely entirely on mines to prevent the co-operation of enemy naval elements with their air elements.

2. Our skies must remain British. We can continue to defend, even though at present the Germans have a huge preponderance of planes; but we shall not be able

to counter-attack until our fighters have driven the German bombers entirely from the skies. The events of the next few weeks will prove whether we can prevent overwhelming damage to our ports, but we cannot at present be certain of always being on the spot where the surprise has been planned.

3. We must so organize our home forces, and behind them our male population, that everything can be done to snuff out the invasion at its most vulnerable moment, which is the very first of all, when the parachutists are landing.

We should see the new tactics of invasion as acting exactly like a small leak in a dyke. If the leak can at once be stopped, the damage will be small; but, unless the first leak is stopped, there will be no stopping the flood later.

It is with the stopping of this first leak that the rest of this pamphlet is concerned.

The Arming of the People

It is not our business to discuss how the Navy, Army, and Air Force should go about their tasks in the defence of Britain from invasion. We, the People of Britain, must organize to stop the first leak before it becomes an overwhelming torrent. We are back in primitive times, when every farmer cultivated his fields with a weapon within reach.

THE ARMING OF THE PEOPLE

We are back to the days when every eye that could scan the seas watched day and night for the sight of a sail, and inland dwellers watched the hilltops for the lighted beacon.

Moreover, a great change has taken place in the relative importance of town and country in the defence of our land. We have thought most hitherto of defending London and our great industrial cities from air bombardment; but now we must concentrate upon the fields and downlands, the little villages, and the isolated farmsteads.

Many of us laughed at the A.R.P. enthusiasms of the small villages; but these will now play an important part in the defence of the country, a more important part, perhaps, than the whole A.R.P. system of London.

Indeed, we can define the necessary answer to the peril of the hour in one sentence: The Time Has Come to Arm the Whole People.

Many patriotic and genial old gentlemen have written to the paper in recent weeks, pointing out that their services have so far not been required, and that this, that, or the other organization of veterans ought to take over the job of repelling the coming invasion.

Certainly all their offers should be accepted; but, until the Nazis are broken, there is nothing for it but to have every householder, every head of a family, armed to protect his own homestead. It may not be necessary to provide a gun for every suburban dweller, or for everyone in the long streets of the East Ends of our great industrial towns; but out in the country it is different. Untold harm may be avoided simply because a farmer happens to have his rook gun by his side at the right moment.

The People of England must be armed in the defence of their life and liberties, and arming does not merely mean possessing something that will go off, and knowing how to make it go off in the right direction.

It means also having an elementary but sufficient knowledge of the tactics required for the particular job which Hitler has forced on us. Even a rabbit can best be disposed of if you have, besides your gun, a dog and a ferret. Even a parachutist sets a task which requires the co-operation of several human beings, each of whom knows what he ought to do, each of whom understands his particular part within the group to which he belongs.

CHAPTER IV

A Nation of Observers

First of all we must study the art of observing. We must not be carried away by fanciful stories of parachutists descending in sky-blue clothes with transparent cellophane parachutes, or disguised as nuns or priests. Nevertheless, we must be on the look-out for the isolated disguised saboteur, who may be dropped from time to time to prepare the way for the real parachute invasion.

What are you to do if you actually see a parachutist descending?

First of all, you should remember that there is a hundred to one chance that the parachutist may be a British airman making a forced landing. It is not very likely that this will be the case; but it is worth while bearing the possibility in mind, especially if you have a tendency to shoot at anything you may happen to see. Frankly, there is a danger at the present moment of people losing their head and imagining that every stranger and every refugee is a disguised enemy. That is why I began with this warning.

Of course, the problem of how to recognize a friendly parachutist can only be solved with the co-operation of the parachutist himself. A British airman bailing out over the British countryside by means of a parachute must on landing do everything he can to call attention to himself.

Parachutes Over Britain

Even so, he must be approached with care. He must be made to put his hands up: he must be searched, and taken for identification to the local authorities; but no amount of enthusiasm for National Defence will justify his being shot in the air before he has had time to make himself known.

In the second place, it must be a hard and fast rule that no one seeing a parachutist descend shall lose sight of him, even in order to warn the nearest military or police authorities. The best thing, if it is possible, is to keep the parachutist in sight, but at the same time to contrive to pass on the information to somebody else, who can in his turn warn the authorities and bring them to the danger point. This is easy, if the parachutist is spotted by a properly organized patrol, for such patrols will always work in pairs for this very purpose.

But it is quite possible that the vital observation will be made by a man, for example, working in the fields. It would be a good thing if everyone who works in the country were to have a whistle with a prearranged whistling signal. In this way it would be possible for a farm labourer to whistle to his wife or to a fellow-worker, whose job would be, first to get a sight of the signaller, so as to be told by dumb show why the signal was given, where the parachutist is, and so forth, and then at once, without approaching the observer, and as

A Nation of Observers

unobtrusively as possible, to go and get in touch with the authorities.

In the third place, the longer the parachutist is unaware that he has been observed, the less likely he is to get away. If it is necessary for the observer to make a sound signal, he should do so immediately he spots the parachute, while the enemy is still in the air and unlikely to notice the sound. He should keep himself completely hidden, and when the parachutist moves, he should use his judgment as to whether he ought to follow, and thereby run the risk of being lost before the defence patrols come up, or get a general idea of the parachutist's probable movements and direction, and stop where he is until the patrol has found him.

He must not hail the patrol with shouts, which would warn the parachutist, but signal silently the approximate whereabouts of the enemy, so that the place can be surrounded.

In the fourth place, the observer should never approach too close to the parachutist, if he has been seen, even though he may be armed with some kind of gun. Unless the parachutist has obviously got a rifle or a machine-gun, it will be safe to come within 500 yards of him, since the kind of automatic weapon that he is most likely to have will certainly not be able to shoot farther than that range.

Parachutes Over Britain

If the parachutist appears to have a longer-range weapon, the most important thing for the observer is to keep hidden.

Sending in Reports

It is not likely, however, that many observers will have parachutists dropping at their feet, or within an uncomfortable distance of them. More often people are likely to see, or think they see, parachutists dropping a mile or so away. It then becomes very important to know exactly how to make a report

It will not be the slightest use for an unarmed, or poorly armed, isolated observer to go chasing off after the parachutist, hoping to come up with him and keep him in sight. What will be much more valuable will be a carefully compiled report of the exact position from which the observation was made, and the exact position of any natural object, such as a hill or a wood, behind which the parachutist was last seen disappearing.

Having very carefully made a note of these particulars, the next thing is to get them to the authorities as soon as possible. Almost always this can be done by telephone, and everybody working out of doors from one end of the country to the other should know at the beginning of the day's work where the nearest telephone is.

Further than this, people like farm labourers, and others with a more or less fixed place of work, should

SENDING IN REPORTS

learn as much as they can about the names and numbers of their fields and landmarks, as they appear on a large Ordnance Survey map. Every enclosed field in England has its Ordnance Survey number.

If you know, for example, that the ten fields on your farm are numbers 512 to 521, and that the wood down the farm lane is called Furnace Wood, all you have to do when you have seen your parachutist is to telephone the authorities something like this: " This is Bill Jones reporting parachute descent. Enemy seen from Field 515 disappearing behind left arm of Furnace Wood."

You must take the shortest possible time to convey your information, because it is very much to be hoped that somebody else is already waiting to phone in from some other telephone number another report about your parachutist: " This is Tom Harris, reporting parachutist descent. Seen from Wood Green crossroads, disappearing behind Collier's Hill."

When your report and Tom Harris's have both come in, all that the officer has to do is to put two rulers along the two pairs of points mentioned in the two reports, note where the lines meet, and immediately have that point carefully surrounded by patrols, who will either close in on the enemy, or watch for an attempted breakaway, whichever seems wisest to the commanders in the particular station.

So much for the proper way of making reports. Now

a word or two as to the wrong way of reporting. It is worse than useless, having spotted a parachutist, to race down the road shouting out the exciting news to any passer-by. The fewer the people who know that a parachutist has come down, the better from several points of view.

First we must avoid causing panic or anxiety. You should regard it as a crime to pass on gossip, true or false, about parachutists, because you may get all the local mothers so worried that they are terrified of sending the children to school.

Second, it is essential that the enemy knows as little as possible about the fate of his parachutists. It is of equal value to the enemy to know that parachutists have made a successful landing, or that they have failed to land. The parachutist may be the forerunner of many others. His instructions may be to reconnoitre a given locality and report by his portable wireless transmitter or some other means as to its suitablility for landing troop-carrying planes: or a small group of parachutists may have been dropped in order to seize a flat field, clear it of obstacles, and prepare it for the landing of planes.

If nobody knows that the parachutists have landed, the enemy is left guessing not only as to what has happened to them, but as to what course the bigger operations for which he was sent to prepare should take.

Nothing could be more heartening to an invading enemy than to know that his parachutists have gained a foothold. To know absolutely nothing about their fate is likely to be more disconcerting than to know outright that they have been captured.

The rule, therefore, for every observer, that is to say, every British adult, is: Make your report accurately and quickly to the proper authority, and then seal your lips. We should get into the habit of so trusting one another not to discuss parachutists that we shall know at once that any gossip that we do hear is likely to be " Fifth Column," or at least irresponsible and untrue. This imposes a great strain on the lucky observer responsible for spotting a parachutist; but he must keep his story for his friends and children when the war is over.

Strangers on the Road

One of the most miserable things about war is that it leads us to suspect every other human being we meet. It is going to be a very difficult task to know how to patrol the roads, especially at night, without making life not worth living for any of us.

The first step will have to be to restrict our movements after dark to what is absolutely necessary, and no more. Of course, if a descent of parachutists is known to have taken place in a particular locality, people may have to be told to keep indoors until the enemy has been rounded up, and in certain vital areas there should be a permanent curfew.

The sort of problem that will arise is this: An unknown number, say twenty parachutists, have been seen to decend at different points within a square mile. Patrols have been drawn round the area; but it is by no means certain that none of the parachutists have got away. What is to be done?

The first thing to do is to put yourself in the position of the parachutists. Why did they land where they did? What will they be anxious to do first? How will they set about doing it?

You will, of course, know roughly the military objectives in the neighbourhood. Most of them will be guarded day and night. Most of them, too, will be unknown to the parachutists, for even German thoroughness cannot possibly succeed in dropping men who know the minute details of the exact locality where they land.

The parachutists will first of all try to ascertain where they are. It is more than likely that they will remain hidden in some wood until the hours of daylight, and then try to mingle with normal traffic, and spread over the country. We must, therefore, do all that we can to make it difficult for them to get their bearings.

In Finland all railway station names were taken down; otherwise it would be perfectly easy for the parachutist

STRANGERS ON THE ROAD

to go straight to the railway station restaurant, order a cup of coffee, and take a glance at the station name. It may be necessary to remove every single signpost on our roads. That will be no inconvenience to the local inhabitants; and by now motoring for pleasure ought to have dried up.

There would have to be in certain cases new signs in code for the use of military traffic, and these would be supplemented by cross-roads patrolmen, who would question very carefully anyone who asked the way.

The second need of the parachutist saboteur will be food. German thoroughness will have provided him with a certain amount of English money; but we can be thankful for our Government's foresight in changing our treasury notes so recently, an action which no doubt will be followed quite soon now by calling in all treasury notes of the old design.

It will, therefore, not be likely that the parachutist can be provided with sufficient unsuspicious-looking money to purchase food for long, and doubtless he will try to live off the countryside, which is not so difficult during the summer months. However, the country is so well prepared to make the disguised parachutist's life short, and not particularly merry, that the danger from this source can easily be over-estimated.

We must remember that the advantages of being able

to drop spies by parachute are considerably reduced in the case of our own country, because in no circumstances could the spies get back with any information they are likely to pick up. Dropping parachutists behind the enemy's lines may be a fruitful source of information on the Continent, but it is unlikely to be so here.

CHAPTER V

Mass Parachute Action

The real danger is not from the isolated, disguised parachutist coming as a spy or saboteur, although these gentlemen seem to have captured the imagination of the man in the street: it is from the use of parachutists in numbers as part of an organized invasion on a large scale. It is action against these that I have called, " stopping the leak."

The danger requires the careful attention of all our armed Home Forces; but the general public has many duties to perform here also. A countryside experienced in the art of street fighting and the building of barricades would be of inestimable value as an aid to the military forces.

Barricades

The first task of the People, as distinguished from the military, should be to slow up the movement of the invaders as far as possible.

Those who have been through the Spanish Civil War know that there is a scientific method of building a barricade, which, and that there is a good deal more to it than piling up the nearest portable obstruction. The most primitive method is simply to block with anything handy half the width of the road, so that wheeled traffic has to go slowly, and so afford a chance for its examination. Such a barricade would not be the slightest use for stopping determined mass parachute invaders, whether advancing on foot or in captured vehicles.

A good barricade will have been built with one eye on the possibilities that the traffic may refuse to slow up, that it will, in fact, try to get through by attacking the guard with automatic weapons. The barricade will, therefore, be more than a mere obstruction; it will be a fortress.

It should, of course, be built, wherever possible, round corners, so as to take the oncoming vehicle or pedestrian by surprise. It should be built in two halves, each of them rather more than half the width of the road, and one half about eight feet further back than the other. In this way no vehicle can possibly rush the gap: it has to stop and thread its way sideways across the road to get through.

Moreover, oncoming vehicles should be covered by soldiers concealed in another direction from those at the barricade, who give the challenge to halt. The halted car must be covered from the flank from the moment that it is forced to draw up.

Then again, it is of no use simply to block the road with a barricade, if no attention is given to the pos-

BARRICADES

sibility of the enemy leaving his vehicle and circumventing the barricade on foot.

A guard, who has been placed at a barricade in a road and told simply to watch oncoming traffic and stop it is likely to find himself in a very bad position, if he is faced by determined invading troops, unless he has either had experience of street fighting, or has had a good training by those who have.

Properly trained parachute invaders moving along a road will have an advance patrol of some sort, and, if on turning the corner the patrol is loudly challenged, the rest of the force will not lose a second before they will have deployed into the fields on either side of the road and taken the barricade in the rear.

A barricade must also be so constructed that it will cause the minimum of delay to one's own motor transport. We want to delay the invading enemy as much as possible; but we must not interfere with our own mobility. In Spain, therefore, the scientific barricade maker very often constructs a part of the barricade in such a way that it can be easily and rapidly removed, when, for example, a supply column wishes to get through without it being apparent to an approaching enemy where the movable or weak section of the barricade lies.

It is to be assumed that every one of the young militiamen and others, who are at the present time

German parachute soldier. Note sub-machine-gun, folding bicycle, portable radio.

employed at the thousands of barricades across our country roads, knows that he may at any moment not merely have to examine strangers and arrest them, if they have not got the proper documentation, but also defend his barricade against the attack of a determined enemy.

Village Barricades

It may happen that a force of parachutists may attempt to occupy some small town or village, and succeed in doing so before an adequate military force can arrive to keep them out. In such a state of affairs the only hope of stopping the leak will be that the village inhabitants shall be organized and instructed as to what they have to do.

Almost every village has already got its volunteers for Home Defence. These must not think that their training consists solely in practising with a rifle and in going on observer patrol. They may have to know how to defend their village streets. They must know how to complete proper barricades, and the proper place in which to build them.

Unfortunately, our history, having been very different from that of the Spanish, gives us very little information on the tactics of street fighting. In Spain almost any villager can tell you the exact street corner where the barricades have always been raised in the past, and will always be raised in the future, in obedience to the same sort of laws of military strategy as condemn Louvain to destruction in any war through Belgium.

If the parachutists are in considerable force it is fairly certain that regular troops will be needed to clear them out of the village, and the barricades of obstruction set up by the volunteers against the parachutists must not be made in such a way that they will later become valuable defences in the hands of the parachutists against the military.

Of course, the first object of building barricades is to avoid the temporary capture of the village by the enemy. Once the enemy has got a foothold in the building it will take a very much greater force to get them out again; and so every effort must be taken to prevent this.

Barricades, therefore, should be built across every entrance to every village in the more vulnerable areas. It may be necessary, in order to maintain national mobility at this stage, to keep the main roads free of obstruction; but all the material should be by the side of the road, ready to hand; and the ideal plan of the barricade fully understood by those who may have to set it up. On side roads barricades should be already in position, and observers be on the watch over any footpaths and other approaches.

Street Defence

The main object of the defenders in street fighting will be first to confine the parachutists into as restricted an area as possible by means of properly contrived fields of fire, second to [obscure their field of vision by " blanketing " the roads down which machine-guns can be pointed against the military when they arrive.

Quite often it is possible to inconvenience a strong and determined force operating in the streets of a small town by this very simple process. A stone attached to a string is thrown across from one side of the street to another, by people standing either on the roof or in upper windows. The string is pulled across, and blankets or sheets attached to it are allowed to hang down, so as to curtain off the whole length of the street from the enemy's sight. The enemy can no longer snipe at anyone walking in the street, and, short of keeping up a continuous machine-gun fire through the blanket, is unable to prevent the use of the street for the purposes of the relieving forces. Of course, such blanketing operations must only be carried out at points which can be defended and, from which the enemy can be observed without his observing you, otherwise you will simply be spoiling your field of vision as well as his.

Another duty of defence volunteers in villages will be to make things as difficult as possible for the parachutists by locking all doors, removing all supplies of food and fuel, thus restricting their movement and setting a limit to the time they can hold out.

A fully worked-out scheme of street defence will take care that immediately upon the warning being given of the approach of a force of parachutists, every inhabitant, having carefully locked every door in their house and removed all stores of food, should at once go to neighbouring points, from which they can be evacuated as easily as possible in case the parachutists have to be bombed out of their positions.

Keep Communications Open

The defenders of the village must realize that it is of the first importance that they remain in touch with the outside world, and they should, therefore, have their local telephone exchange and telegraph office not merely guarded, but sandbagged and generally put in a state to stand a siege.

But, since telegraph and telephone wires still run so often overhead, and, are therefore, easily cut, every village should have its trained despatch riders able to

KEEP COMMUNICATIONS OPEN

get out of the village by some path or other, even if the invading force succeeds in cutting all the road approaches.

We must emphasize here, something which will have occurred to the reader again and again, namely, that the whole essence of successful defence against invaders by parachute or otherwise must be a dependence on one's own local unit for the defence of one's locality. It is of no use waiting for some organization centred in Whitehall or elsewhere to give instructions. Successful defence of a village depends first and last on being in the hands of those with intimate knowledge of the village and the country immediately surrounding it.

The central authorities responsible for Home Defence, have very wisely given a fairly free hand to local government groups in the organizing of their defence This is the right approach ; but it makes it essential that every town and village in England should have a realistic idea of the sort of problem they may have to face locally, and should work out the strategy and tactics required to deal with those problems.

It is necessary for every local group to realize that they may find themselves, for a time at least, cut off from the outside world. Lord Woolton recently made

PARACHUTES OVER BRITAIN

the welcome announcement that food storage had been so decentralized that there were depots in 800 different places. This splendid piece of organizing must be backed up by detailed preparation to prevent a breakdown of supplies. Thus, every local committee responsible for the defence of a village should make sure that there are enough supplies in the village for everyone for a week or ten days, in case something serious occurs.

Of course, nothing serious will happen to more than a few dozen of Britain's thousands of towns and villages. The trouble is that nobody can say beforehand which few dozen will be singled out.

The whole art of successful defence rests in assuming that your own household and your own village must be as well prepared for an emergency as any other household or village in the country.

Guard Against Troop-carrying Planes

We must always keep in mind that parachutists are not merely spies and saboteurs coming in small groups to cause damage and confusion : they are far more likely to be the forerunners of larger invading forces brought by transport planes. We must not neglect to prepare for these also.

The essence of our new danger of invasion is that

GUARD AGAINST TROOP-CARRYING PLANES

no longer need the invaders come by sea to our ports, which they cannot do so long as we have our navy, and coastal defences intact : they can now come out of the sky wherever planes can land. Any flat piece of England which can be seized by parachutists and controlled by them long enough to get rid of obstacles to landing, is a possible danger spot.

We must, therefore, increase to the limit the obstacles to safe landing on every likely piece of flat land. There are many ways of doing this. The principal is the same as that of laying a minefield. We cannot sow the whole sea so thick with mines that it is inevitable that a ship sailing anywhere will strike one ; but we can lay sufficient mines to make the danger not one which is worth risking. We cannot cover every piece of flat country in England with obstacles ; but we can make landing a very hazardous task.

An airport can be very quickly rendered useless either by driving vehicles on it and arranging them so that there is no free runway ; or by destroying its surface with bomb craters. A good size field with crops can be rendered very dangerous by stretching lengths of cable a few feet above the surface of the ground, or by driving in stakes.

Parachutes Over Britain

Wherever it can be done without impeding agricultural operations, large fields and other open spaces can be made dangerous by parking any old farm implement that can be spared as plane traps over the area. It may be advisable to use a good many of our park railings as plane traps, rather than melt them down for iron. Every farm has a remarkable amount of material lying about, which can be used in this way. Even cattle can be distinctly dangerous for landing planes.

Naturally, the first flat spaces to receive attention should be those dangerously near objectives likely to be of value to an invading force.

Of course, if the original leak reaches the proportion of a torrent of transport planes, matters cease to be controllable by the People, and we have to rely on the military arm to dispose of them.

We shall by then have found ourselves faced with an army in our midst, armed probably with light tanks and light howitzers. Doubtless we shall still be able to deal with them ; but it is the duty of the People of England so to assert themselves now that they are prepared to stop the leak long before it grows to a torrent.

Invasion and the War as a Whole

It is always necessary to keep things as far as possible

INVASION AND THE WAR AS A WHOLE

in perspective. This is particularly difficult with the threat of invasion, which is now upon us. Naturally the feeling that our own homes, our families, our children may be going to receive a frontal attack from the forces of evil tends to dwarf everything else that is happening.

Let us remember, therefore, one thing. This war is not going to be lost by the annihilation of a large part of the British Expeditionary Force, nor by the landing of invading armies, nor yet by the wholesale destruction of our towns. Germany will only win the war if these masterpieces of brute force prevent us from using the tremendous advantage we have over Germany, of vastly greater economic resources.

What has happened is this. The Nazis, by depressing the standard of living of the people of Germany through many years, have succeeded in accumulating a big store of raw material, of oil, of armament. During the same period, because of the downright slackness of our political leaders, we have failed to accumulate anything like such great stores.

For the moment, therefore, we are at a great disadvantage. That is why we have lost so heavily in Flanders. But we must remember this. It is not going to be possible for Germany to replace the incredible mountains of armaments and floods of oil that

PARACHUTES OVER BRITAIN

have been used against our men in the most terrible battle in the history of the world.

We, on the other hand, have woken up. Now that we are awake we are able to build up our strength.

We do not know whether the Germans, to gain their first great victory, have lost so great a quantity of supplies, that they will have to pause before attempting the next part of their programme but we do know that they have lost so much that the invasion of England is bound to be their last desperate throw.

We are not even yet their equals in planes, in tanks, in armaments generally ; but, if we can force them to continue using up their stores at anything like the rate of the hideous weeks of May, then within three months the whole balance of strength will have tilted in our direction.

Foresight would have prevented the coming trial, the coming partial destruction of our cities, the coming defilement of our countryside. We must pay for lack of foresight ; but, unless we allow ourselves to be broken by this great trial, there is no possible way for Germany to win the war.

By the time these words can be printed two or three new dangers may have arisen. We may have new

Invasion and the War as a Whole

enemies to fight: we may see France still further beleaguered. But the basic assumption behind what the Nazis have done is that our nerves will not be able to stand punishment.

We are an old and worn-out people, they say. We have certainly lived too comfortably, probably, as a nation, to keep in perfect training; but we, too, have a *secret weapon*—the spirit of a nation of free individualists, who were not forged into a battle weapon by vicious propaganda and a reign of fear, but by a knowledge of what we have to lose, and an understanding of what we are fighting for.

> " God gives all men all earth to love,
>   But since man's heart is small,
> Ordains for each one spot shall prove
>   Beloved over all.
> Each to his choice, and I rejoice
>   The lot has fallen to me
> In a fair ground—in a fair ground—
>   Yea, Sussex by the Sea ! "

In July 1936, I saw the villagers of Spain building their barricades across the village streets, and chalking up the words: " They Shall Not Pass." They did pass. All that is an old, sad story, whose pages cannot be reopened now.

In May 1940, I saw the Sussex villages surrounded with barricades, and I saw evacuated children marching proudly up the village street behind young armed men in armour.

The battle between right and wrong is more clearly seen now, and this time " They Shall Not Pass." And an old spirit has risen into men's hearts once again ; we are called upon to defend the cottages of Burwash, the pavements of Lambeth Walk, the cliffs of Dover, the fens of the east country. The People of Britain has risen in its armed strength.

Artist's fantasy of 50 years ago. Troop-carrying balloons drop Scots parachute-kilties.

MATTERS OF MOMENT

This is the first of a series of booklets on front page subjects to be published for "MOMENT" by the Pilot Press.

First-class authors will provide the public with the most authoritative information on matters of MOMENT.

First-class illustrations will be a notable feature of a series invaluable to everyone.

Appearing Shortly

RUMOUR

by Ivor Lambe

www.ingramcontent.com/pod-product-compliance
Lightning Source LLC
Chambersburg PA
CBHW040312050426
42450CB00020B/3465